TRUMPET

MAKING ♪ MUSIC

KATE RIGGS

CREATIVE ℂ EDUCATION

PUBLISHED *by* Creative Education
P.O. Box 227, Mankato, Minnesota 56002
Creative Education is an imprint of The Creative Company
www.thecreativecompany.us

DESIGN AND PRODUCTION *by* Ellen Huber
ART DIRECTION *by* Rita Marshall
PRINTED *in the* United States of America

PHOTOGRAPHS *by*
Corbis (Andrew Kent, Chris Stock/Lebrecht Music & Arts),
Dreamstime (Polojig), iStockphoto (Rodrigo Blanco,
Yuriy Chaban, Scott Dunlap, eROMAZe, Horst Gossmann,
Ela Kwasniewski), Shutterstock (Yuri Arcurs, aricvyhmeister,
Sergei Bachlakov, Horatiu Bota, fotum, Arunas Gabalis,
Gabrielav, Anton Gvozdikov, vadim kozlovsky, Ela Kwasniewski,
Anita Patterson Peppers, PhotoHouse, Edwin Verin),
Veer (MarFot)

LIBRARY OF CONGRESS
CATALOGING-IN-PUBLICATION DATA
Riggs, Kate.
Trumpet / Kate Riggs.
p. cm. — (Making music)
SUMMARY: *A primary prelude to the trumpet, including what the*
brass instrument looks and sounds like, basic instructions on how to play it,
and the kinds of music that feature it.
Includes bibliographical references and index.

ISBN 978-1-60818-370-8
1. Trumpet—Juvenile literature. 1. Title.

ML960.R54 2013
788.9'2—DC23   2013009499

FIRST EDITION
9 8 7 6 5 4 3 2 1

TABLE OF CONTENTS

WHEN YOU HEAR A TRUMPET

Car horns blaring.

A clear, cold night. Buzzing bees.

Geese honking as they fly.

What do you think of when you hear a trumpet?

Busy bees make buzzing sounds.
Geese honk loudly at each other.

THE BRASS FAMILY

Musical instruments that sound and look alike belong

to a "family." Trumpets are part of the brass family.

Brass instruments use air to make sounds.

A brass player blows air into a cup-shaped mouthpiece.

mouthpiece

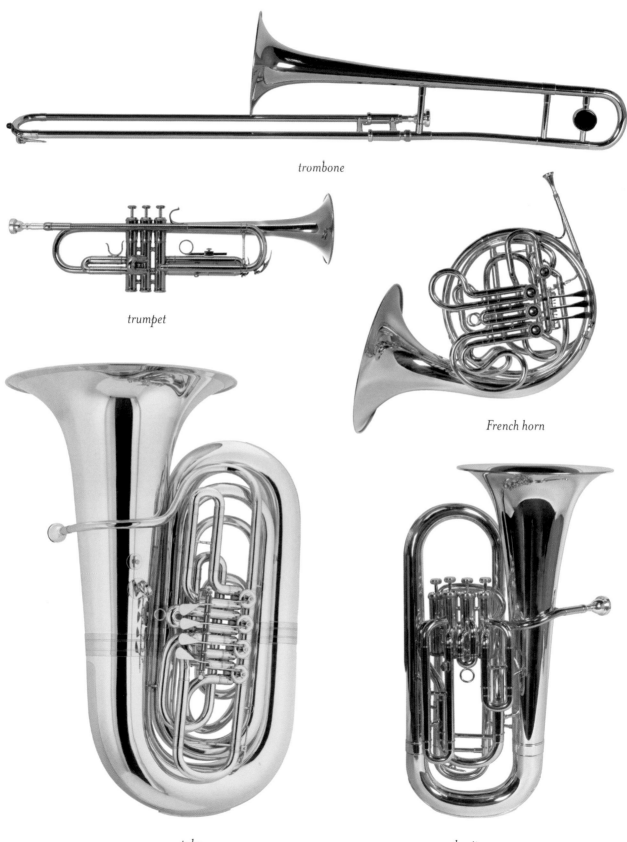

trombone

trumpet

French horn

tuba

baritone

mouthpiece

bell

A trumpet's pipe would be 4.5 feet (1.4 m) long if it were unwound.

PARTS OF A TRUMPET

The mouthpiece is on one end of the trumpet.

The **bell** is at the other end. A pipe loops around from

the mouthpiece to the bell. A trumpeter can change

a trumpet's sound by putting a mute in the bell.

Three common mutes are the straight, cup, and wow-wow.

The wow-wow mute makes a silly "wah-wah" sound!

The wow-wow mute (pictured) is also called a Harmon mute.

SLIDES AND KEYS

The leadpipe goes from the mouthpiece to

the **tuning** slide. A small part called the water key is

under the tuning slide. The hot air from a

trumpeter's breath collects inside the trumpet.

A trumpeter pulls the water key to let water out.

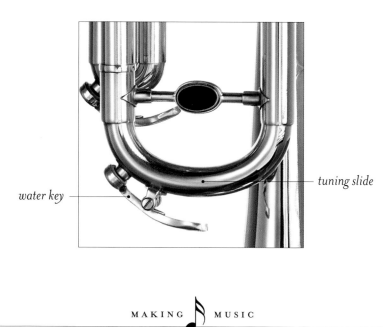

water key

tuning slide

If too much water collects inside a trumpet, it makes a crackling sound.

Pads underneath the valves help soften the noise they make when pressed.

KINDS OF TRUMPETS

A trumpet has three valves that the musician

presses to make different notes.

The tops of the valves look like buttons.

Most trumpets are 18 to 22 inches (46–56 cm) long.

Bass trumpets are the largest trumpets.

Trumpets are made of metal and can be gold- or silver-colored.

PLAYING THE TRUMPET

You hold the trumpet with your left hand.
You squeeze your lips against the mouthpiece.
Then you blow into the mouthpiece, **vibrating** your lips!
Use the fingers on your right hand to press on the valves.

The left hand can change the tuning slide while playing.

Trumpet players have to keep their lips tight and buzz to make a sound.

This valveless trumpet was made in Germany in 1598.

EARLY TRUMPETS

Trumpets have been around for hundreds of years.

People used trumpets long ago during battles and hunts.

They also used them to play fanfares. These are songs

that announce when someone important is coming.

The first trumpets with valves were made in the 1800s.

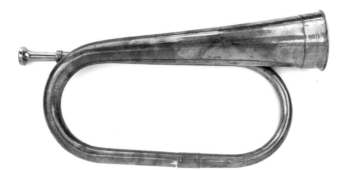

military bugle

TRUMPET MUSIC

Many trumpeters play in bands and orchestras

(*OR-keh-struhz*). Brass bands are made up

of only brass instruments.

Jazz bands and big bands play special kinds of music.

A trumpeter plays with guitarists and other musicians in a band.

Trumpets make good marching band instruments because their sound carries well.

A TRUMPETER PLAYS

A jazz trumpeter stands next to the microphone.

He takes a big breath and blows into the trumpet.

The rest of the band plays along.

People get up to dance to the trumpet's brassy sound!

A trumpet's bright, powerful sound makes people want to dance.

Wynton Marsalis was born in 1961. He grew up

in New Orleans, Louisiana. He loved playing trumpet

when he was a kid. He played with many bands, orchestras,

and other groups. Then he started his own

band when he was 20. Wynton **records** *a lot of music.*

His CDs have won many awards. Wynton also likes to

write music and teach people about jazz.

Wynton Marsalis plays on a Monette trumpet made just for him.

GLOSSARY

bell: *the wide end of a trumpet that flares out*

jazz: *a type of music that uses fast, bouncy rhythms; it started in America in the early 1900s*

records: *makes a CD or tape of something that can be played later*

tuning: *fixing the pitch, or sound, of an instrument*

vibrating: *shaking or moving up and down rapidly*

READ MORE

Ganeri, Anita. *Brass Instruments*.
North Mankato, Minn.: Smart Apple Media, 2012.

Levine, Robert. *The Story of the Orchestra*.
New York: Black Dog & Leventhal, 2001.

Nathan, Amy. *Meet the Musicians: From Prodigy (Or Not) to Pro*.
New York: Henry Holt, 2006.

WEBSITES

Dallas Symphony Orchestra Kids
http://www.dsokids.com/athome/instruments/mouthpiece.aspx
Have an adult help you make your own mouthpiece from a soda bottle.

New York Philharmonic Instrument Storage Room
http://www.nyphilkids.org/lockerroom/main.phtml?
Learn more about trumpets, and listen to one play!

Every effort has been made to ensure that these sites are suitable for children, that they have educational value, and that they contain no inappropriate material. However, because of the nature of the Internet, it is impossible to guarantee that these sites will remain active indefinitely or that their contents will not be altered.